TUGGING ON YOUR HEARTSTRINGS

Written by Award Winning Poet
Margaret High

Copyright © Margaret High 2021
High Margaret
Tugging on Your Heartstrings
All rights reserved. The use of any part of this publication reproduced, transmitted in any form or by any means electronic, mechanical, photocopying, recording or otherwise stored in a retrieval system, without the consent of the publisher, is an infringement of the copyright law.

Self-Published
Margaret High
Cambridge, Ontario

For more Information
E-mail: *margaretehigh@gmail.com*

Facebook Pages
@authormargarethigh
@myjustncase

ISBN 978-0-9809826-7-1

Dedication
I dedicate this book of poetry to those who
have experienced, love, loss, and abuse hardship,
broken heart, broken dreams,
Hope his book will be an inspiration
and tug on Your Heartstrings
Take a quiet moment sip on your favourite
glass of wine or cup of tea
"Oh, don't forget the tissues "

Table of Contents

Memories of Home 1
Christmas on the Island 2
A Memory Etched In Time 3
My Special Place 4
My Grandma Didn't Care 5
For Being the Dad You Didn't Have to Be 6
These Are My First Footprints 7
A Mothers Journey 8
Link to the Past 9
Treasured Moments 10
Once Stood With Pride 11
To My Daughter with Love On Mother's Day 12
Dear Santa Claus 13
To the Daughter I Never Knew 14
To Our Son on His Wedding Day 15
To My Son and His Wife On their Wedding Day 16
Confirmation Day 17
To our Grand Daughter 18
Happy Father's Day Dad 19
My Second Mom 20
Teenager 21
Memories That Never Die 22
Wasted Youth 23
How are you Today 24
Eve's Story .... 25 & 26
Why? 27
Why did you Choose Me 28
Innocence 39
Words to my Daughter 30

Table of Contents

Mom and Dad 31
Taking Care of God's Garden 32
In Memory of my Daughter 33
Covid 19 34
Reflection 35
Thank You So Much 36
Friends 37
Nature's Flower 38
First Love 39
The Gift of Love 40
Happy Birthday to my BFF 41
I'll Think of You 42
Dangers of the Grand 43
Sisters 44
We are Connected 45
Life is too Short 46
Crossing Guard 47
I...Appreciate 48
You are so Beautiful 49
911 "Disaster" 50
A Letter to the Terrorists 51

Memories of Home

Blowing winds, whistling among the cliffs
Waves make a lullaby song against the shore
The salty sea air, so crisp and clean
"Ah, who could ask for anything more?

Walks along the rocky beach
And across the barren hills
Ocean stretching out touching the sky
This breathtaking view can give you chills

Fields and fields of wildflowers
Waving friendly in the breeze
How small and insignificant you feel
Standing underneath those tall pine trees

Fishing boats bobbing on the deep blue sea
Seagulls anxiously hovering above
The enormous whales peeking up to spray
Memories...of the homeland that I love

Yes, Newfoundland has all these things
Cliffs, the shores, the salty crisp air
And friendly people to welcome you
I'm so proud I came from there

Christmas On the Island

Christmas on the Island
It was a special time for me.
Hills and snow-covered valleys,
Surrounded by the sea

These times of years gone past
Bring memories to mind
When mothers stayed home and cooked
While fathers worked in the mines

Wealth was something known by few
As we scrimped to save each year
To bring a little Christmas
To our family and our friends so dear

The tradition was a part of our heritage
carried down from parent to child
Not forgetting the meaning of Christmas
I often think of it... and smile

Our stockings were hung on the bedpost
With only the fewest of treats
Filled with apples, oranges and grapes
And maybe, some candy for sweets

Our presents were things that were needed
Homemade mitts scarves and hats
To keep us warm from harsh winters
And we were happy to be getting just that

Yes... Christmas on the Island
Was a special time for me
Never having much in material things
Yet...we were as wealthy as can be

A Memory Etched in Time

He was a farmer a fisherman, a tinkerer of sorts
Worked as a miner deep under the ground
He was gentle and quiet ne'er a harsh word
Men like him were hard to be found

I felt very safe when by his side
There were never any kisses or "I love yous"
He wasn't one for showing emotions
But somehow you just knew

He showed his caring in so many ways
Like making things with his hands
Toys furniture things that were needed
With little education, he drew up the plans

A special memory comes to mind
While working with him one day
Chopping down trees for firewood
For the long winters coming our way

As we sat on an old tree stump
He picked the trees to be cut
He handed me some cold black tea
Served in an old tin cup

He said "Son we have lots of work to be done"
As he rolled his cigarette
Without looking my way he handed me one
It was a feeling I'd never forget

That day he made me feel like a man
Just quietly sitting together
This memory of my father and me
It Will live in my heart forever

My brother told me about the first time our father found out he was smoking I wrote this poem as a gift to my brother.

My Special Place

As a child, I'd go wandering
On a bright summer's day
Through a field of buttercups
And smell the new-mown hay

I took a path down through the woods
Soft damp moss at my feet
I took a sip from a babbling brook
The water was cool and sweet

As I continued on my way
Taking in the beauty around me
The morning dew fell like baby's tears
Trickling down from an old tall tree

I came upon an open field
The sun shone on my face
I saw the prettiest ocean view
There lies my special place

I heard the seagulls' mournful cry
I saw boats bobbing in the bay
I sat on a blanket of tall green grass
On a bright summer's day

We all may have a special time or place. This special place for me is in Newfoundland, Canada, on a little island called Bell Island. Its beauty leaves a lasting memory in my mind.

My Grandma Didn't Care

I dropped some crumbs on grandma's couch
Her Rug her bed the car
I jumped up on the table
and gave her quite the scare
I lost my socks and broke the dog dish
Her cookies she would share
I'd run around in my bare feet
My grandma didn't care

I dropped some milk on the floor
My PJs have a snare
My face is such a sticky mess
I leave my toys everywhere
Even when she's much too busy
She still makes time to spare
I leave a mess all over
My grandma didn't care

I play hide and seek
I hide behind the chair
I sometimes have an accident
And mess my underwear
And when I stay the night
She helps me say my prayers
Even If I forget
My grandma didn't care

Now that I'm all grown
The visits I know are rare
I often think about
The memories that we shared
The fun we had at grandma's
How she was always there
And the love she gave us
Yes... my grandma really cared

I am blessed with three grandsons Justin and Cody and Connor. When they were little and I had them for the weekends at my house was always a mess but I didn't care I just loved spending time with them all including my Great Grandchildren.

For Being the Dad You Didn't Have to Be

Thank you for being the Dad
You didn't have to be
For letting me into your heart
And taking good care of me

The day you came into my life
I thank the Lord above
For sharing special memories
And fill my life with love

Dad, we've shared so many things
Throughout my childhood years
We shared a lot of laughter
And yes even shared some tears

Dad, I wrote this poem
To show how much I care
And to say "Thank You"
For always being there

These Are My First Footprints

These are my first footprints
Though tiny they may be
To keep inside a picture book
As a m-e-m-o-r-y

They may be tiny now
But watch me as I grow
Leaving mud upon your carpet
And footprints in the snow

I will travel many miles
In just one single day
Exploring many obstacles
That lay there in my way

At the end of each new day
Until tomorrow a brand-new start
As I lay sleeping like an angel
I'll leave footprints in your heart

A Mother's Journey

The journey into motherhood
Isn't easy to achieve
My love for you grew deeper
From the moment you were conceived

As I felt you grow inside me
My anticipation grew as well
Was it going to be a boy or girl?
I could hardly wait to tell

Then one day it happened
You came into this world
My anticipation ended
A beautiful baby girl

There is no special book
That guides us on which way to go
Just a mother's instinct
And love is all you know

It was my responsibility
To teach you right from wrong
And lead you in a direction
To grow up loving wise and strong

You may not have always agreed with me
One thing I know for sure
My love, it still grows deeper
The more that you mature

You probably won't understand these things
Or why it has to be
But I could only teach you
The way it was taught to me

Parenting is not an easy job children need to know they are loved and parents have a responsibility to show as much love as they can.

Link to The Past

When my father passed away
I was in my early teens
It left me divested
And shattered all my dreams

As I went through his belongings
I found a scarf I put aside
Keeping it as a memory
I often wear it with such pride

This scarf has seen many perils
Keeping me warm throughout the years
Sharing in my laughter
And absorbing some of my tears

It may be a little tattered
His fragrance still lingered there
Leaving a calmness over me
And feeling his presence near

It's a link back to my childhood
Sweet reflections that will last
Like the strands within my father's scarf
Linking the future with the past

Now I have children of my own
When they come to understand
I'll share with them my father's scarf
And the meaning of each tattered strand

My sister-in-law told me about her father's scarf she wore I wrote this poem for her as a birthday gift.

Treasured Moments

There are many treasured moments
Mom We remember as a child
Your patience and understanding
You're caring and your smile

We may not have understood
The hardships you've gone through
You had a way of protecting us
Cause that's what you would do

The aromas of home-cooked meals
Family gatherings in our home
With the friendly ringing of laughter
We would never feel alone

You've done more than your share Mom
Taking us back home when we needed to mend
Helping us whenever possible
Not just as a mom but also a friend

There were problems but "you" overcame them
And at times you were unsure
But time is the greatest healer
With your strength, you have endured

Mom you have given us a legacy
Of integrity strength and love
And to be blessed with you as a mother
We thank the Lord above

Done with love for you Mom

Once Stood with Pride

This house once stood with pride
Chimney smoke bellowing
Children's laughter, echoing
Family dog howling

This house once stood tall
Flowers wafting fragrance
Colourful splendour radiance
White picket fence

This house once in its prime
Held stories and nursery rhymes
Babies cry's and mothers' tears
Holding secrets and fears

This house now abandoned
Once bright, now dark and cold
Cracked paint, and overgrown
The walls hold stories...yet to be told

To My Daughter with Love On Mother's Day

I thank the Lord above
For a daughter such as you
For your sweet and caring ways
And the special things you do

Reflecting on your childhood
And memories I hold so dear
I cherish every moment
And I'll always keep it near

I'm proud of you my daughter
Of the mother, you turned out to be
The joy you bring your children
Is there for all to see

We have a special bond
That only mothers know
The memories that you'll share
As you watch your children grow

You'll have a better understanding
Of the joy that they will bring
That the very word "Mother"
Becomes a treasured thing

Wishing you all the joy
And love on Mother's Day
That you have brought to me

Love Mom

Dear Santa Claus

Dear Santa Claus Could you please come
To our house, Christmas eve
It's just my baby brother,
My mommy, and me

We don't have lots of money
To buy a lot of things
And we'll be very happy
With whatever you may bring

We'll brush our teeth
And go to bed for mom, real early tonight
We'll hang our stockings, on the bed
And close our eye's real tight

On Christmas morning, like magic,
Presents filled the Christmas tree,
Some for my brother and mommy,
And a big one just for me.

We are so very lucky
Merry Christmas every one
"Oh Santa Claus, oh Santa Claus "
I knew that you would come

Christmas is such a magical time for Children

To the Daughter, I Never Knew

I made a terrible mistake
I was young and didn't know
I never realized the impact
Of having to let you go

I never got to hold you
To kiss you or say goodbye
I always think about you
I still often sit and cry

I had a choice to make
It was the hardest thing to do
I pray one day you'll forgive me
Because I was only thinking of you

I was young just a teenager
With no one to help me through
Scared and all alone
I felt this was the only thing to do

If God would grant me just one wish
I pray to the Lord above
One day I could let you know
How much you are truly loved

I was inspired to write this poem after listening to a co-worker talk with great pain about the Daughter she had to give up at birth.

To Our Son on His Wedding Day

Just yesterday you were in our arms
So tiny and so sweet
Our hearts were filled with love
You made our lives complete

The journey into manhood
Was not an easy road to take
But we are so very proud son
Of the choices that you've made

As you stand there on your wedding day
A tear falls down my cheeks
It's just old memories flooding by
Of a baby so tiny and sweet

We'll always be there for you
No matter where you may roam
And please remember son
Our love still remains at home

So, to our dearest son
We would like to say
We wish you happiness and love everlasting
On this your wedding day

Love always

To My Son and His Wife
On Their Wedding Day

In my heart, he'll always be "My Little Boy"
But today he stands a man
If I shed a tear today
I hope you understand

A mother's heart holds memories
I may sometimes cling to the past
Forgive me if I seem a little sad
For he's grown up much too fast

I raised and loved this little boy
But today my son takes your hand
I'm proud as any mother can be
Proud of this grown young man

Promise me you'll always love him
From now and all your life
I will let go of this little boy's hand
As you take it... as husband and wife

Wishing you only the best
Love you always

Confirmation Day

Your parents picked a name for you
the day that you were born,
They baptized you in the house of God,
And kept you safe from harm.

They did the best that they could do
In teaching, you which way to go
And gave you the tools you need
And a spiritual way to grow

Now today is your Confirmation Day
Confirming the things you were taught
You're old enough to choose the path
That may bring you closer to God
I
hope the choices that you will make
When you journey, into Manhood
Will take you down a wondrous path,
In his miracles, you can see the good

A little poem for my Grandson
on his Confirmation Day

To Our Grand-Daughter

You came into our lives
On a beautiful summer's day
You were so wanted
More than words can say.

You had all your fingers and toes
Your skin so milky white,
When you came into this world
"Oh", what a beautiful sight

As grand-parents, we feel so lucky
We thank the lord above
To have another grand-daughter
To kiss, to hold, to love

We'll watch you as you grow
We'll be there whenever we can
And if you stumble and fall
We'll be there, to hold your hand

And on your child-hood journey
We'll help you along the way
Whatever we can do
You only have to say

Happy Father's Day Dad

Dad... You're always in my heart
And have been a part of my world
As a grown-up woman
Or as daddy's little girl

Dad... Fond memories come to mind
When I was just a child
Of the happy times together
I remember them and smile

Dad... You're always on my mind
Each and every day
All the love, I have for you
Is shown in my special way

Dad... This day is special,
And it's just for you
I hope to share some memories,
That is special, for just we two

With love

To My Second Mom

I know you're not my birth Mom
You are as good as any Mom could be
You were there for me through the years
Helping, nurturing, and guiding me

You were more than just a second
Mom You were like my" bestest" friend
A bond that we have shared
I hope will never end

When I had questions about life
You answered as best you could
And when I had difficult times
You truly understood

In my eyes, you are my Mom
You gave me a warm and loving home
And with a sense of belonging
I've never felt alone

Just a little Thank You
For all that you have done
Mom...in my heart
To me, you are number one

Teenager

Like a butterfly leaving its cocoon
Ever-changing spreading their wings
From a child to a teenager
Chosen paths and curious things

Young carefree expressing themselves
Knowing more than experience in years
Rebellious minds with a passion
Receding from their peers

The closeness you once felt
Becomes foreign and not of the mind
Expectations you once had
It may happen but only in time

All that matters is here and now
Fun and friendship seem to reign
The responsibility falls to the bottom
As parents struggle to maintain

Love a passionate emotion
Thinking they have found "the only one"
Without them, they could not go on
Into this journey, they have begun

Armed with patience and time
Praying maturity and wisdom will appear
Like the changing of a butterfly
Turning life's full circle it all becomes quite clear

The changing moods of a teenager inspired me to write this poem.

Memories That Never Die

The sweet sound of a whippoorwill
Breaking silence in the trees
Wildflowers waving
In the warm summer breeze
Sailboats in the harbour
Rocking softly with the tide
These are memories that never die

A kaleidoscope of colours
Covering the ground
Paint the prettiest picture
No artist has ever found
Trees are standing naked
Dark clouds fill the sky
These are memories that never die

Turning back the pages
Of Christmas so long ago
Children's laughter ringing
With the first fall of snow
Smells of Christmas baking
Mom's homemade apple pie
These are memories that never die

Seasons come and go
Like a chameleon, they change
Bringing all the wonders
Mother Nature has arranged
Time goes by so slowly
Since evolution, we've wondered why
These are memories that never die
These are memories that never

Wasted Youth

Youth is wasted on the young they say
At times I tend to agree
Do they know we once were young
Strong vibrant and carefree?

We once had sweethearts that loved us
And children we raised with care
All we ask in return from our families
As we age that they'd always be there

We once had friends that we hung with
Old age took them one by one
Our families have grown and deserted us
Now feeble alone and shunned

The clock on the wall ticks the seconds
Every second seems like days
We do nothing but remember the past
And our young and carefree ways

Enjoy your youth; too fast it's gone
And you are where I am today
Living with nothing but memories
Watching as time ticks away

How Are You Today?

"How are you today?"
The storekeeper lady said
Does she care to know
Of the thoughts going around in my head?

Does she care I'm all alone
No one to share my day?
Does she care sometimes I feel
I'm only in the way?

Does she care my pace is slow
As people quickly pass?
Sometimes I feel confused
But nobody takes time to ask

Does she care I come to her store
Just to pass the time?
Does she know the challenge it takes
For each step, I have to climb?

When you ask" How are you today?"
Please say it as if you care
And I will feel your sincerity
And how I am I will gladly share

Sometimes when we ask the question without thinking
"How are you today?" do we care to know.

Eva's Story

I was only three years old
When my innocence was taken from me
The scars I now will carry
Will change who I could be

As a child, I felt unworthy
I could never do anything right
I tried so hard to please
For someone to hold me tight

"You'll never amount to anything"
And abuse was all I knew
There were no hugs or kisses
There were no" I love yous"

The man that I would marry
Forced himself on me
Carrying his child inside
A loveless marriage my destiny

The horrors that I've endured
The beatings I had to bare
Feeling scared and all alone
Oh, why didn't somebody care?

continued on page 26...

continued from page 25...

My only salvation
Were my children that survived
To protect and keep them safe
Was my reason for staying alive

When I look into their eyes
Finally, I did something right
They are my life my everything
I thank God for them each night

God has sent his miracles
Through people that truly cared
And has especially touched my life
No longer alone and scared

I kept the promise that I'd made
So very long ago
My children have been safe
And loved because I tell them so

The scars that I have carried
Plays like a movie in my head
Rather than turning it off
I choose to tell my story instead

I was inspired to write this poem for a lady that was badly abused from the time she was a child her story was heartbreaking.

Why?

Why is it that victims
Are sentenced to serve a lifetime?
While the criminals are set free
To continually repeat their crimes

I live a life sentence
Each and every day
Of the pain that's been inflicted
While you go on your merry way

Why didn't someone protect me?
From the harm that you have caused
What is wrong with our system?
What's wrong with our laws?

They are caught they're brought to justice
And here where things go array
The criminals have all the rights
While the victims have to pay

So why do we have laws
Why give the criminal the rights?
Why not protect the victim
And keep them safe at night

There is so much sexual abuse in this world.
The victims are never quite the same.

Why Did You Choose Me?

Why did you choose me?
You shattered my whole world
Ripping me of my purity
I was a youngster, a young boy or girl

Why did you choose me?
I was a happy innocent child
You stole the spark from my eyes
My lips no longer smile

Why did you choose me?
Why not someone your age
With your sick and twisted mind
Inflicting your pleasure and your rage

Why did you choose me?
You changed who I became
Filling me with emptiness
Fear, guilt and shame

Why did you choose me?
I now have a story of survival to tell
Of how I took back my power
And came back from the hobs of hell

Why did you choose me?
Why not just pass me by?
Consider for just one moment
There would be one less life... you would destroy

Innocence

Hopscotch, Kick the Rock
Hula-hoops and lollipops
A sweet time of innocence
Where...has it all gone?

Special glances, first romances
Teenage dances, taking chances
Passion rising ever so high
Not knowing what's in store

Wedding bells, bride and groom
Keeping house, starting roots,
Baby's crying, needs attending.
Love is dead and gone.

Broken dreams, broken hearts,
Children's pain, lonely hours,
Hopscotch, Kick the Rock,
Hula-hoops and lollipops.

A sweet time of Innocence,
Where...did we go wrong?

Words to My Daughter

I may not have carried you inside me
But I carried you inside my heart
I chose you as my daughter
Nothing could keep us apart

I felt so lucky to have had you
And I thank the Lord each day
Having you as my daughter
Has meant more than words can say

I dreaded you finding your birth-mom
It was always my greatest fear
I felt a little threatened,
Worried you'd no longer care

Forgive me if I made you feel guilty
Or seemed distant from time to time
Fear can do many things
Losing you was forever on my mind

I love you so very much
I only wanted the best for you
But, I should have had more faith
You always knew the right thing to do

You have been a wonderful daughter
And have been there right till the end
Thank you for all you have done
Now it's time... for your heart to mend

I will be in a better place
Where there is no darkness or pain
Filled with God's glorious love
Where only peace and tranquillity reign

So... go on and live your life
Enjoy as much as you can.
One day we'll be together
One day you'll understand

A friend of mine wanted to leave a message to her adopted daughter. When she found out she had cancer, she had a chance to give her daughter this poem, I wrote this just for her.

Mom and Dad

Mom, I'm sending you a dream
On the pillow where you lay your head
Of restful days not heartbreaks
And of wondrous times ahead

I am in a better place
Where there is no sorrow or pain
A place in God's glorious kingdom
Where only peace and tranquillity reign

Dad, I'm with the angels
Competing in a race of some kind
With that old, familiar adrenaline rush
Crossing that finish line

Oh yes, I hug my children
And kiss them every night
I'm that little whisper of silence
After they turn out the light

For I am all around you,
In all the beauty you see,
When you stop to smell a rose,
Take some time and think of me

There is no blame on anyone
My path was in God's hands
He called me to His home
Someday... you'll understand

Mom and Dad, I send this dream
Of peaceful nights and love
I know we'll be together
In God's heavenly home above

This poem was written for a couple from Texas. Their daughter died at the hands of her husband it was a murder-suicide. She was very active in sports and left behind two small children. Writing this tugged in my heartstrings.

Taking Care of God's Garden

Mommy and Daddy, I'm okay
I'm in heaven up above
God sent His angels to greet me
And oh... how I feel so loved

God gave me a special job to do
It's special because He told me so
He said my smile brings the sunshine
And it helps his garden to grow

God showed me His beautiful garden
Such beauty I'd never seen
I sit with the angels and ponder sometimes
It is so peaceful and serene

Yes, I miss you, Mommy and Daddy
But I'm around you every day
I hear you when you think of me
And I hear you when you pray

We will see each other when it's time
Someday you'll understand
We all will be together
It was always in God's plan

The loss of a child is devastating. I hope this poem will be an inspiration to some parent.

In Memory of My Daughter

You took her home too soon Lord
I didn't want to let her go
She was my all, my everything
"Oh" how I miss her so

She was like an angel
Her smile would warm your heart
We knew she was a special gift
Right from the very start

Oh, how she loved to learn
She liked the arts, and nature of any kind
She stayed at home just to help me
Without complaining ...she didn't seem to mind

She volunteered for many organizations,
And won awards, for her devotion
Her heart was as big as the sky
And as calm as the waters on the ocean

She was very educated
But you would never know
She was never one to brag
Or to ever let it show

I know when it's time for me to go
She will be waiting with, arms opened wide
When once again, we'll be together
Forever ...side by side
Until we meet again
Love, Mom.

COVID 19

In 2020 the world would change
It would never be the same
A deadly pandemic hit us
COVID 19 they named

This virus was like no other
It took millions of lives
It took senior's, sons and daughters
Husbands and wives

It was so very contagious
It kept families and friends apart
You couldn't hug or say good-bye
To our loved ones who departed

It causes chaos and confusion
At Hospitals and Nursing Homes
It closed down businesses
When it will end is still unknown

Wearing a mask and keeping a distance
Would be our daily routine
Streets and parks were empty
It became an eerie scene

If something good would come from this
Is that we love each other more
Recognize the ones who still worked
During this crazy uproar

We appreciate the sacrifice
For all those that had a job to do
While fighting this deadly virus
From the bottom of our hearts a big "Thank You"

Reflection

As I sit here in isolation
Reflecting on what has come
Staying away from loved ones
Trying to keep Positive, and staying home

We take so much for granted
Our Doctors, our Nurses, and our healthcare
So many risk their lives
While you're at home, they still have to be there

From here on in
This world will never be the same
It's not a time for Hatred
It's not a time for blame

We are all in this together
Feeling the same stress and pain
Every country has lost loved ones
They will never see again

The world may have its differences
Political views may not be as we believe
But the commonality of this virus
We all have suffered and Grieved

Thank You So Much

Words cannot express
How grateful I am to you
For the time you spent with my parent
And for the special things you do

They say there are angels among us
I know, I've met a few
But the ones that work at a time like this
Facing dangers, you never knew

You may never get the credit
That you so rightfully deserve
And for choosing to keep working
Even if the virus, has not reached the curve

To me you all are Angels
With a special job to do
Taking care of our loved ones
Even, after all, you go through

So from the bottom of my heart
Thank you for being you
May God keep you all safe
And keep doing what you do

Friends

We have been friends now
Friends for many years
We have shared a lot of laughter
And yes, we've shared some tears

You've been there for me
When things were good and bad
We've celebrated the happy times
And you've helped me through the sad

We've had our ups and downs
But our friendship remains strong
We always come together
No matter who's right or wrong

When I'm feeling down
You know how to make me smile
And if I needed you
You'd walk a hundred miles

That's what makes friends special
And you are special to me
I hope our friendship continues to grow
Like the branches on a tree

Nature's flower

The flower, one of nature's best
Is there for all to see
Reaching upward towards the sun
Enhancing its beauty

The petals, unique in their way
Clustered tightly together and yet
Each is its own, a separate entity
As precious as the droplet of sweat

The leaf, green, sometimes jagged
Clings to a single stem
It's there as an extension
Like the cut on a brilliant gem

The earth is its foundation
To protect, nurture, its task
Against many perils of nature
Delicate as a fine piece of glass

An astounding array of colours
Sets the tapestry for nature's bouquet
It started from a lonely seed
And its beauty ... is there on display.

First Love

"You Don't Forget your First Love"
They will always be in your heart
There may be many reasons
Why...you drifted apart

Maturity may be one reason
You were way, much too young
Perhaps you were unsure
If they would be the one

Parting ways, you move forward
Eventually, meet another
You marry, have a family
A new life to discover

But often you would wonder
About the one, you left behind
Could they have been the one?
So often crosses your mind

Do they ever think of me?
Would they regret letting me go?
Did they ever really love me
I guess we'll never know

The Gift of Love

God gave to me a gift of love
I had to give away
But every time I tried
Close to my heart, it stayed

I gave it to my husband
He took it so easily
He knew he couldn't keep it
So he gave it back to me

I gave it to my children
They kept it for a while
Then they gave it back to me,
With a kiss, a hug and a smile

I gave it to my grand-children
To share in their own way
But they just gave it back to me
So in my heart, it stayed

So, I just gave it to the Lord
He smiled and said to me
This is a gift I gave to you,
It just keeps going around ... you see

I was inspired when I felt blessed with the gift of love, from my husband, children and grandchildren.

Happy Birthday to My BFF

I wanted to get you something different
Unlike any store-bought card
Something to express my feelings
Something from my heart

From the first time that we met
I had a feeling that we'd be friends
There is a special bond between us
I hope that never ends

We've shared each-others laughter
And felt each-others pain
Through all of life's tribulations
Our friendship still remains.

At times I feel we're like Thelma and Louis
Running off to who knows where
Just kicking back and having fun
Without any worries or care

You've always been there when I needed you
Any time night or day
And I've always cherished our friendship
It means more than words can say

What gift can you give a friend
But to say what's in your heart?
I can say it better in a poem
Much better than a card...

I'll Think of you

Your journey now has ended
And I must walk alone
God waits for you at Heaven's Gate
To lead you to your home

I'll think of you when the morning sun
Feels like warm hands touching my face.
I'll think of you when eagles fly
Gracefully into space

I'll think of you when a summer's breeze
Touches my lips like a kiss
I'll think of you when a newborn cries
You once were a part of all this

You'll be there in all the beauty
In things that are old and new
When I stop to touch a rose petal
At that moment I'll be thinking of you

I'll think of you when I walk on a beach
Leaving footprints in the sand
Wishing yours were there beside me
Holding each other's hand

But I know I must carry on
To live life as full as I can
Someday we'll be together
It's all in the Master's plan

I wrote this poem for a friend that lost her husband.

Dangers of The Grand

Two more people lost their lives
From the rapid waters of the Grand
One was just a very young boy
The other, a family man

Children are warned of the dangers
But they play there anyway
A strong current pulled the young boy down
He was the first to lose his life that day

They couldn't get his body out
A police diver went in to try
Never thinking for a moment
That he'd be the second one to die

Crowds gathered from all around
Growing bigger with each day
Waiting with anticipation
Will they bring them both home today?

Some were there for curiosity
Some to give a hand
And some to teach their children
The dangers of the Grand

Policemen serve the community
In many various ways
Giving their lives for others
Not expecting any praise

To me, this policeman was a hero
And not just a family man
So take a moment to say "thank-you,"
Whenever you pass the Grand

I was inspired to write this poem while listening to the news one day. A boy drowned in the Grand River and a diver went in to retrieve his body when the unspeakable happened: The diver also lost his life.

Sisters

As sisters, we share many things
We were close as any two sisters could get
But time and life got in our way
And that's something I regret

We shared clothes, we shared secrets
We shared laughter and tears
Had we'd kept in closer touch
We would not have missed so many years

We shared our childhood memories
Some were happy some were sad
At times when we felt alone
Each other was all we had

But Sis it's not too late
To get back to where we used to be
To rekindle our family ties
And build memories between you and me

I miss you and love you
Your Sister

We are connected

We are all connected, we are born
We breathe air, we see, we hear
We touch, we taste, we smell

We live, we feel, we care
We protect, we nurture,
We love, we hate
We feel pain, we bleed

We communicate
We learn, we grow
We procreate, we create, and we destroy
We age, we grow feeble.. we die

We are all connected
We are one

Life Is Too Short

Life is just too short
To be spending it in doubt
To worry about what might have been
And what life is all about

Enjoy the comforts you have now
And be good to all mankind
You will find more happiness
And live with peace of mind

Don't waste your life with bitterness and hate
Just fill your heart with love
And live life's precious moments
Give thanks to Him above

Thank Him for the wondrous things
You see and do each day
And do these things as best you can
Because life---is a very short stay

Crossing Guard

Mommy, who is that crossing guard
And why is he dressed like that?
He's waving at passers-by
And he's wearing a funny hat

Honey ... he's an angel
Sent here to make us smile
He wears that funny hat
To put a gleam in the eyes of a child

He waves at passers-by
To brighten up their day
And stops the ongoing traffic
So they can go safely on their way

We watch for him each day
As we drive slowly by
It does our hearts good to see him
Now... do you understand why?

Yes, honey, he's an angel
Sent here to make us smile
We hope he'll be our crossing guard
For more than just a while

There was a crossing guard on Homer Watson in Kitchener who would often dress up to make people smile. He would always put a smile on my face. He told me that he loved to see people smile as they drove by and that he loved his job.

I... Appreciate

I appreciate feeling good more
When I'm feeling bad
I appreciate feeling happy more
When I'm feeling sad

I appreciate truth more
When I hear a lie
I appreciate a miracle more
When I hear a newborn cry

I appreciate the sun more
On a cloudy day
I appreciate the word more
When there's something good to say

I appreciate a friend more
When I feel alone
I appreciate kindness more
When a kind act is shown

I appreciate peace more
When countries are at war
I appreciate tolerance more
When freedom of privileges is restored

You Are So Beautiful

As a child, I felt so ugly
No confidence, no reason to smile
Abused, and pushed aside
Not feeling that I was worthwhile

Until one blessed day
A lady stood by my side
She said, "You are special and so beautiful,"
I thought I would burst with pride

I looked into my mirror that day
To see the things, she saw
I saw I wasn't so ugly
I studied myself in awe

This lady was an angel
She changed who I became
By saying I was beautiful and special
I no longer felt the shame

Now I will spend the rest of my life
Telling every child, I see
You are special and so beautiful
Because it had such an impact on me

I was inspired to write this poem when Oprah Winfrey told her fans about a lady that said kind words to her and how it changed her life

911" Disaster"

It was just another day
On an early September morning
When unspeakable disaster hit
Hit us without any warning

Buildings, which once stood proudly
Now crumbled to the ground
Impacting with a deadly force
This followed by an exploding sound

Many lives were lost that day
Lost in the name of hate
Never suspecting for a moment
That this would be their fate

Out of rubble came heroes
From many walks of life
Policemen, firemen, and loved ones
Someone's husband, child, or wife

As the world watched in horror
History was made that day
Many hugged their loved ones
Many just silently prayed

You may destroy a great symbol
You may also take many lives
But you will never destroy the spirit
Our freedom of choice will survive

I wrote this poem after the 911

A Letter to The Terrorists

We died on September the 11th
The year two thousand and one
The world watched in horror
At the deed that you have done

But the terror that you've inflicted
Backfired as you know
It has pulled the world together
We see the love and respect they show

We see nations pull together
To fight for what they believe
To keep our rights and freedoms
That we fought for and achieved

We see a new respect for policemen
Firemen, volunteers and such.
People stop to say thank you,
Because of the lives, they've touched

We weren't fighting for any cause
When you took our lives that day
We were innocent family people
Not a threat in any way

To our friends and family
Hate has torn us apart
You were foremost in our thoughts
We said good-bye to you in our hearts

Inspired by 911

www.ingramcontent.com/pod-product-compliance
Lightning Source LLC
Chambersburg PA
CBHW011614290426
44110CB00021BA/2595